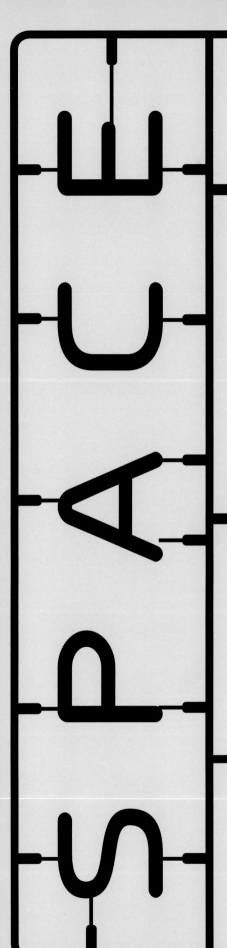

SPACE

ADVENTURES IN
STEAM

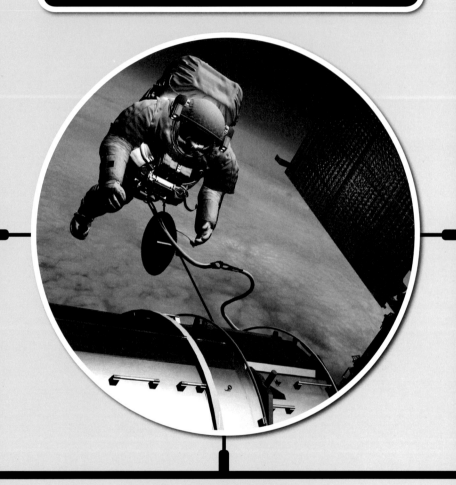

Richard Spilsbury

CAPSTONE PRESS
a capstone imprint

Fact Finders Books are published by Capstone Press,
1710 Roe Crest Drive, North Mankato, Minnesota 56003
www.mycapstone.com

Library of Congress Cataloging-in-Publication Data

Library of Congress Cataloging-in-Publication data is available on the Library of Congress website.
978-1-5435-3236-4 (library binding)
978-1-5435-3548-8 (paperback)
978-1-5435-3554-9 (eBook PDF)

Summary: Take a trip into space and discover the spacecraft, satellites, and telescopes that travel among the galaxies and stars. Learn about the astronauts who have lived in orbit and set foot on the moon and find out about the future of space tourism and exploration.

Editorial Credits

Series editor: Izzi Howell
Designer: Rocket Design (East Anglia) Ltd
Illustrations: Rocket Design (East Anglia) Ltd
In-house editor: Julia Bird

Photo Credits

Julian Baker: 11 and 45l; NASA: 3, 5t, 6, 12, 17t, 17b, 18t, 18c, 18b, 19t, 19c, 20, 22, 23, 24, 26, 27, 29t, 29b, 30b, 35b, 37, 39, 42, JPL-Caltech 5b, 36, 38, Pat Corkery, United Launch Alliance 10, Bigelow Aerospace 21, Dmitri Gerondidakis 31b, ESA, and the Hubble Heritage Team (STScI/AURA) 33, CXC/M.Weiss 34t, JHUAPL/SwRI 34c, JPL-Caltech/UCAL/MPS/DLR/IDA 34b, JPL-Caltech/MSSS 40, 41t, MSFC 43, MarsScientific.com and Clay Center Observatory 45; Shutterstock: iurii cover and title page, RJ Design 7, Jorg Hackemann 8, Everett Historical 9, 28, 30c, 31t, 31c, Andrey Armyagov 14, Harvepino 15, Delpixel 25, AuntSpray 30t, MarcelClemens 32, Belish 35t, solarseven 35c, ESB Professional 41b; Wikimedia: RIA Novosti archive/Alexander Mokletsov / 19b, Jeff Foust44.

All design elements from Shutterstock.

First published in Great Britain in 2017 by Wayland

Printed and bound in China at WKT Company Ltd.

TABLE OF CONTENTS

BEYOND OUR PLANET

WHEN WE LOOK UP, WE SEE CLOUDS AND SKY, BUT BEYOND EARTH'S **ATMOSPHERE** LIES THE MYSTERIOUS REALM OF SPACE. FAR FROM OUR PLANET ARE MANY OTHER PLANETS. SPACE INCLUDES STARS AND MANY MORE OBJECTS, FROM **ASTEROIDS** AND **COMETS** TO **BLACK HOLES**.

The Earth is one of the planets circling, or orbiting, a star we call the sun. Together they are called the solar system. The sun is a massive ball of burning gas, hot enough to warm our planet even though it is millions of miles away. It is just one of a vast number of stars clustered in our **galaxy**. The universe is made up of billions of such galaxies and the large gaps in between objects. These gaps contain nothing but floating dust and gases.

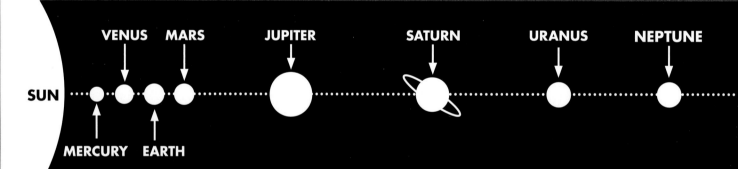

SUN MERCURY VENUS EARTH MARS JUPITER SATURN URANUS NEPTUNE

Planets in our solar system range in size from Jupiter, which is over 300 times larger than Earth, to Mercury, which is less than half Earth's size. The four planets closest to the sun are warm, rocky planets. The outer planets are giant, cold, spinning balls of gas.

" MATH TALK

An astronomical unit (AU) is the distance from Earth to the sun, which is 93 million miles (150 million kilometers). Scientists need larger units called light years to measure the universe. One light year is the distance light travels in one year, or 5,878,792,849,757 miles (9,461,000,000,000 km). The universe is around 93 billion light years across! "

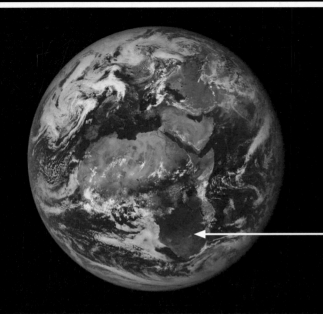

People have been fascinated by and studied space for centuries. In time, they use more advanced technology, from simple telescopes to complex **sensors** on spacecraft. Some lucky people have even visited and experienced space and had the chance to look down on their home planet from above.

THINKING OUTSIDE THE BOX!

In 1931 Belgian priest and scientist Georges Lemaître proposed a new idea. He said the universe started with one giant, incredibly hot explosion around 14 billion years ago. He called it the Big Bang. In the 1960s astronomers finally found proof for the Big Bang theory. They detected **radiation** in the universe that could only be explained as the leftover energy from the explosion.

! SCIENCE TALK

Most scientists now agree that the universe was born from a dot of matter far smaller than a pinhead. During the Big Bang, it suddenly expanded outward. Over millions of years, stars, planets, and other objects formed. Scientists know the universe is still expanding today because galaxies are getting farther away from Earth and each other.

The galaxy containing our solar system is called the Milky Way because light from stars makes it glow white in the night sky. This picture is a nearby galaxy of a similar shape to the Milky Way.

GETTING TO SPACE

AFTER CENTURIES OF WONDERING WHAT IT WOULD BE LIKE TO GO TO SPACE, HUMANS STARTED TO MAKE TRIPS THERE FROM THE 1960s ONWARD. THE CHALLENGES OF REACHING SPACE THEN, AS NOW, WERE ALL ABOUT OVERCOMING THE POWERFUL **FORCE** OF **GRAVITY**.

Gravity is the downward pull toward Earth or other large objects. The pull of gravity on your body, for example, makes you come back down when you jump up. Weight is a measure of the force of gravity on any **mass** (measure of amount of matter). To rise through the air, any aircraft needs to produce a push or **thrust** upward greater than its weight to escape gravity's pull. To lift heavy spacecraft, all space missions have produced the massive thrusts needed with rocket engines.

The earliest rockets were fireworks made from hollow bamboo pieces packed with gunpowder. Lighting the gunpowder created thrust by shooting hot gases downward. But the direction of these and later missiles was inaccurate and hard to control. Fast forward to 1926 when scientist Robert Goddard tested the first modern rocket. Goddard's rocket flew fewer than three seconds and rose just under 41 feet (12.5 meters). But it demonstrated a technology that would be developed into space rockets.

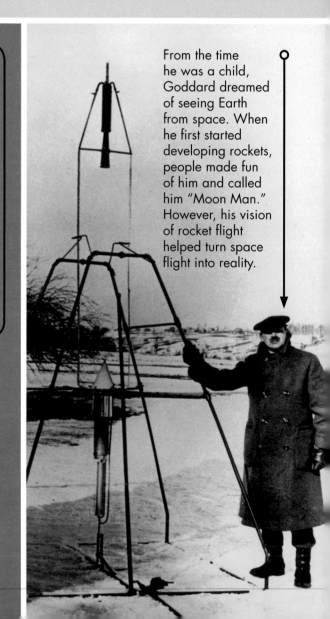

From the time he was a child, Goddard dreamed of seeing Earth from space. When he first started developing rockets, people made fun of him and called him "Moon Man." However, his vision of rocket flight helped turn space flight into reality.

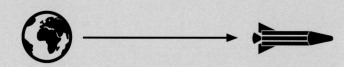

SCIENCE TALK

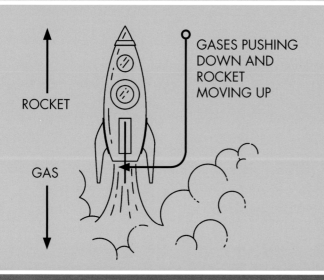

ROCKET

GAS

GASES PUSHING DOWN AND ROCKET MOVING UP

Forces always work in pairs. This is called action and reaction. The action of gases pushing downward causes a reaction in the opposite direction, and so the rocket is pushed upward. Goddard's rocket used liquid fuels of gasoline and **oxygen** in a combustion chamber to achieve liftoff. These provided a more controlled thrust than solid fuels because a certain amount could be burned at a time.

TECHNOLOGY TALK

Goddard improved his rocket design by adding technology. He developed vanes that were connected to a gyroscope in the rocket's nose. These tools helped guide the rocket and keep it stable in flight. He also used a parachute that would deploy once fuel had run out to slow the fall of the rocket back to Earth. All of these technologies have been used on space rockets and other flying machines ever since.

MATH TALK

Solid fuels in Goddard's time gave rockets a two percent efficiency of converting the energy in fuel into thrust. Goddard's design improvements, including using a specially shaped nozzle for gases, raised the efficiency to 63 percent. Even today's rockets can rarely achieve more than 70 percent.

THE FIRST SPACE ROCKETS

DURING THE 1950s, THE **SOVIET UNION** AND THE UNITED STATES WERE ENEMIES AND WANTED TO OUTDO EACH OTHER. ONE WAY TO DO THIS WAS TO GET AN ASTRONAUT INTO SPACE BEFORE THE OTHER. THIS COMPETITION BECAME KNOWN AS THE SPACE RACE.

The V2 rocket was controlled by signals. Although the rocket was sent along a determined path, the signals could command the steering to move the fins near its base.

The rocket showed its power in World War II (1939–1945) when German forces rained down V2 rockets onto London. These liquid-fueled rockets were launched from Germany. Then they flew 49.7 miles (80 km) high in the air and exploded upon reaching their target in the United Kingdom. The Space Race happened because each side realized such powerful rockets could carry not only bombs, but also astronauts and spacecraft into space. In 1942 the first German rocket reached space.

After the war, German scientists involved with V2 development teamed up with Russian and U.S. rocket engineers. They helped build the first space rockets for each side and achieved many more firsts:

 OCT. 1957 ➔  **APRIL 1961** ➔ ⭐ **MAY 1961**

The Soviet Union launch a new Semyorka rocket to put the first ever satellite, *Sputnik 1*, in space.

The *Vostok-K* rocket launches Soviet astronaut Yuri Gagarin to become the first man in space.

The U.S. *Redstone* rocket reaches space, but it is not powerful enough to get U.S. astronaut Alan Shepard into orbit.

The liftoff of *Apollo 11* on a Saturn V rocket in 1969. The Saturn V rocket was 364 ft (111 m) tall and capable of carrying more than 53 tons (48 tonnes) to the moon. It had a total of 10 engines for thrusting it through Earth's atmosphere. It remains the largest space rocket ever built.

THINKING OUTSIDE THE BOX!

The first living things to reach space from Earth were fruit flies in 1947. Ten years later, a dog became the first mammal to orbit our planet. Scientists used animals to learn about the dangers of takeoff and high-speed flight and time in space before humans made the trip.

ENGINEERING TALK

The first design for the *Sputnik 1* **satellite** was too heavy for the existing launch vehicle to lift into space. So Russian space engineers reduced its size and weight. Rocket engineers need to carefully consider the weight of the **payload** when deciding on the amount of engine thrust a rocket needs. The payload is what a rocket carries, such as equipment and astronauts.

★ FEB. 1962
The more powerful *Atlas* rocket takes U.S. astronaut John Glenn into orbit.

★ DEC. 1965
Two U.S. astronauts spend two weeks in space.

★ JULY 1969
A Russian N1 rocket capable of traveling to the moon explodes on the launchpad, causing the largest explosion in the history of

★ JULY 1969
American astronauts complete the first moon landing during the *Apollo 11* mission.

REACHING SPACE TODAY

TODAY'S ROCKETS OR LAUNCH VEHICLES COME IN MANY SIZES, DEPENDING ON THE PAYLOAD THEY NEED TO CARRY INTO SPACE. THE LARGEST ARE CALLED HEAVY-LIFT VEHICLES, WHICH CAN CARRY OVER 55 TONS (50 TONNES) INTO SPACE. SMALL-LIFT VEHICLES CAN CARRY 2.2 TONS (2 TONNES) AT MOST.

Space rockets are **streamlined**, with a long, thin shape that helps them move faster through the atmosphere. Objects moving forward through air are pushed back by it, and this **friction** reduces their speed. A streamlined shape reduces the surface area for air to push against. Smooth sides also reduce the friction or **air resistance (drag)** between air and the rocket's surface.

MATH TALK

Only around 1 percent of a rocket's weight is its payload. Most of the rest is the **propulsion** system of engines and fuel. For example, the launch vehicle Ariane weighs nearly 882 tons (800 tonnes) at takeoff. Of this, 606 tons (550 tonnes) is solid fuel in the boosters, which is used up in the first two minutes of flight.

A rocket needs to be tough enough to withstand massive vibrations from the engines while they fire. The inner frame is formed from vertical beams attached to hoops up the length of the vehicle. A smooth metal skin is shaped around this frame. Both are made from strong but lightweight metals such as aluminum alloys. In parts, such as the tip and fuel tank, the skin is covered with special carbon fiber heat shields. These reduce the heating of the skin and contents from friction.

Many launch vehicles, like Ariane V, have several stages or parts used for different legs of the journey to space.

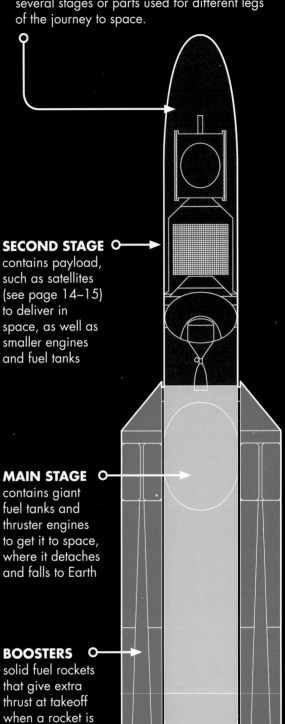

SECOND STAGE contains payload, such as satellites (see page 14–15) to deliver in space, as well as smaller engines and fuel tanks

MAIN STAGE contains giant fuel tanks and thruster engines to get it to space, where it detaches and falls to Earth

BOOSTERS solid fuel rockets that give extra thrust at takeoff when a rocket is at its heaviest, before detaching and falling into the ocean

THINKING OUTSIDE THE BOX!

Engineers are designing launch vehicles that are not rockets. One idea is to use a tough balloon with **helium** to lift a small launch vehicle. The vehicle fires its **thrusters** about 20 miles (32 km) above Earth. Another idea is to use a maglev train on an upcurved track to launch a type of space plane. Maglevs use the push of magnets against each other to lift trains above tracks, eliminating friction and increasing speed.

PROJECT

Design an **aerodynamic** rocket to carry a payload of passengers.

- What source of thrust would you use?
- Why might you need tail fins at the end?
- How would you adapt the design to carry a heavier payload?

IN ORBIT

SPACE BEGINS AROUND 62 MILES (100 KM) ABOVE EARTH'S SURFACE. THERE, THE FORCE OF GRAVITY FROM EARTH IS WEAKER THAN ON THE PLANET'S SURFACE. THERE IS ALSO SO LITTLE AIR THAT DRAG IS MINIMAL. SPACECRAFT CAN **ORBIT** EARTH USING VERY LITTLE THRUST AND FUEL.

Spacecraft manage their orbits using small thrusters. The thrusters are controlled by computers that nudge them left or right, faster or slower. This ensures spacecraft remain at the right speed and height above Earth.

Moving in orbit around Earth relies on gravity. Without it, a rocket would continue outward on a straight path to outer space. Gravity's pull changes the craft's straight motion into a circular orbit. When you throw a ball hard, it travels straight for longer before arcing to Earth than if you throw it softly. In the same way, spacecraft need to move fast to stop gravity from dragging them back toward our planet. Spacecraft orbit at different heights from Earth to avoid flying too close to each other. Those orbiting closer to Earth need to go fastest because gravity's pull is stronger.

SCIENCE TALK

The force of gravity is very strong. Space launch vehicles must reach a speed known as **escape velocity** to break free of its pull. This is at least 24,855 miles (40,000 km) per hour. Once in orbit, a craft must continue to fly at around 16,777 miles (27,000 km) per hour to prevent it from gradually being pulled back to Earth.

Spacecraft are not the only man-made objects orbiting Earth. There are thousands of pieces of space junk. These orbiting objects include parts of exploded rockets, disused satellites (see pages 14–15), and tools or gloves accidentally dropped by astronauts. Space junk is hazardous because it can fly into, and even punch a hole through, a spacecraft in orbit.

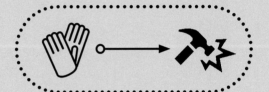

ENGINEERING TALK

Engineers are thinking of solutions to deal with space junk. CleanSpace One is a satellite that hunts down disused satellites in orbit and uses a folding net to pick them up. Then both satellites head toward Earth. Other ideas include stretching out tough fishing nets between spacecraft to trap junk and using special sensors. The sensors spot and track junk movements so that spacecraft can get out of its way.

SATELLITES

ON A CLEAR NIGHT, YOU MIGHT SEE A DOT OF LIGHT SLOWLY CROSSING THE DARK SKY. THIS MIGHT BE AN ARTIFICIAL SATELLITE ORBITING IN SPACE. THERE ARE THOUSANDS OF ARTIFICIAL, OR MAN-MADE, SATELLITES ABOVE EARTH THAT HELP US IN MANY DIFFERENT WAYS.

Some satellites take pictures of Earth to help meteorologists predict weather patterns or allow geographers to make maps. Some take pictures of the sun, other planets, black holes, or distant galaxies to help scientists understand space. Other satellites send TV signals and phone calls around the world.

SCIENCE TALK!

TV and phone signals travel in straight lines, so sometimes they can get blocked by mountains or tall buildings. Today, TV signals and phone calls are beamed up to satellites, which instantly send the signals back down to different locations on Earth.

Some satellites are battery powered but most are fueled by solar panels. Solar panels convert the energy in sunlight into electricity. Satellites have antennae to send and receive data, such as phone messages and navigation instructions. They also have sensors to check that they are facing the right way and small rocket thrusters to adjust their direction.

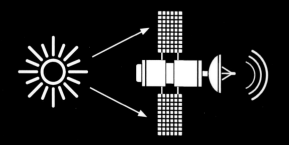

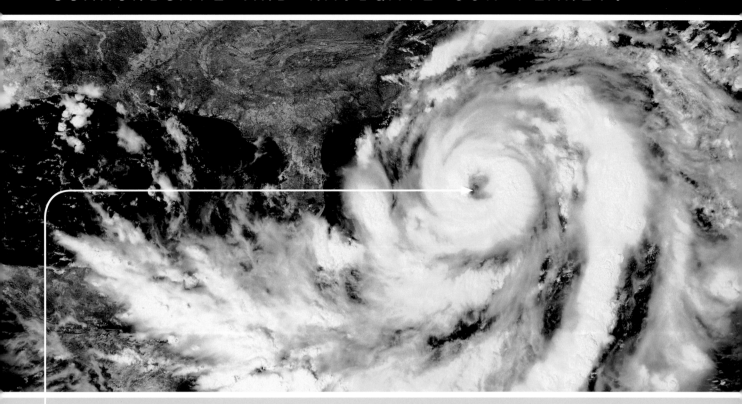

Weather satellites have cameras that take images of clouds and beam them to weather stations on Earth. Meteorologists can use images, like the one shown here of a hurricane, to track its movement and warn people in its path to get to safety.

Global Positioning System, or **GPS**, satellites help us find out exactly where we are on Earth. Each satellite transmits information about its position and the time. GPS receivers determine how far away each satellite is based on how long it takes for the signals to arrive. They use this information to pinpoint your location.

MATH TALK

GPS receivers work by trilateration. Let's say you are on a hill with three satellites in space above. Calculating your distance from satellite 1 tells us you must be located somewhere in the red circle. If you calculate distances from satellites 2 and 3 as well, your location is where the three circles intersect.

THE MOON

THE MOON IS EARTH'S CLOSEST NEIGHBOR. IT IS A NATURAL SATELLITE THAT TAKES ABOUT A MONTH TO ORBIT OUR PLANET. IT IS THE ONLY OBJECT IN OUR GALAXY THAT HUMANS HAVE SET FOOT ON.

The moon probably formed about 4.5 billion years ago from debris thrown into space after a big object crashed into Earth. Unlike Earth, the moon has a thin, weak atmosphere. This atmosphere cannot protect it from the extreme heat of the sun. Nor can it hold on to the sun's warmth to stop it from freezing at night. The moon is airless, waterless, and lifeless.

SCIENCE TALK

The moon is much smaller than Earth but it is large enough to have a gravitational force that affects our planet. The oceans rise and fall in tides because the moon's gravity pulls the oceans that are directly below it.

ART TALK

During the moon's orbit of Earth, the sun only lights up the side of the moon that faces toward it. Its appearance changes as the angle at which we see the moon changes over the month. We may see a crescent, full, or half moon, for example.

The first men to walk on the moon landed there in the *Apollo 11* spacecraft in 1969. Spacesuits provided them with air and protected them from the sun's harmful radiation. They explored the moon's surface for more than 21 hours, taking videos and photos and collecting 48.5 pounds (22 kilograms) of rocks to study on Earth.

Gravity's pull on the surface of the moon is one-sixth of Earth's. This is why astronauts look as if they are bouncing across its surface rather than walking. Without rain, wind, or water to erode the astronauts' footprints, they will probably stay there forever!

THINKING OUTSIDE THE BOX!

Astronauts on the Apollo missions left reflectors on the moon. Scientists bounce a laser off these reflectors and measure how long it takes for the beam to reach Earth again. Using their knowledge of the speed of light, they can work out the distance between the moon and Earth to within inches (centimeters).

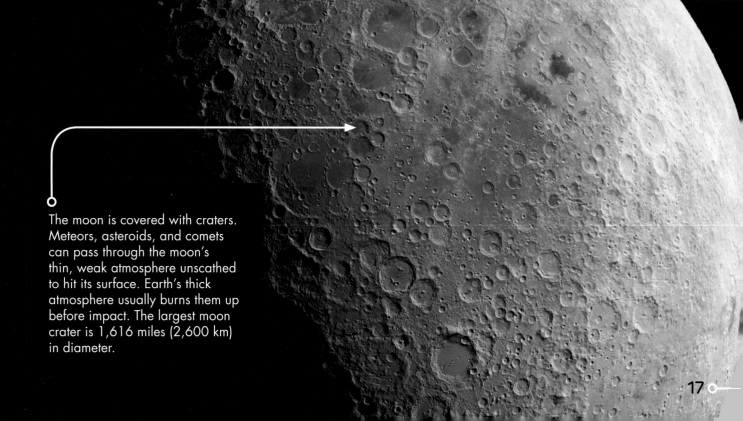

The moon is covered with craters. Meteors, asteroids, and comets can pass through the moon's thin, weak atmosphere unscathed to hit its surface. Earth's thick atmosphere usually burns them up before impact. The largest moon crater is 1,616 miles (2,600 km) in diameter.

MOST OF THE DISCOVERIES AND ACHIEVEMENTS MADE IN SPACE WOULD NOT HAVE BEEN POSSIBLE WITHOUT ASTRONAUTS WHO PAVED THE WAY. BRAVE MEN AND WOMEN TOOK PART IN THE DARING AND DANGEROUS EARLY FLIGHTS INTO SPACE. THESE ASTRONAUTS TRAVELED INTO SPACE WITHOUT KNOWING THE RISKS TO THE HUMAN BODY OR IF THEY WOULD EVER RETURN TO EARTH.

YURI GAGARIN (1934–1968)

Yuri Gagarin was a fighter pilot who became the first human in space on April 12, 1961. His *Vostok 1* spacecraft orbited Earth at 17,026 miles (27,400 km) per hour. At his highest point, he found himself about 203 miles (327 km) above Earth. Gagarin died in a crash at the age of 34 after a routine plane flight went wrong.

JOHN GLENN (1921–2016)

John Glenn was the first U.S. astronaut to orbit the Earth. His 1962 flight made the United States a serious contender in the Space Race with the Soviet Union. In 1998, at age 77, he became the oldest astronaut when he flew onboard the space shuttle *Discovery*. His mission was to take part in experiments on the effects of living in space on older people.

NEIL ARMSTRONG (1930–2012)

Neil Armstrong was the mission commander on the 1969 *Apollo 11* flight to the moon. It was during this mission that he became the first person to walk on the moon. He famously said, "That's one small step for (a) man; one giant leap for mankind." With fellow astronaut Buzz Aldrin, he spent more than 21 hours on the moon, studying the surface and collecting rocks.

JAMES "JIM" LOVELL (1928–)

Jim Lovell made four space flights and spent over 700 hours in space. He is most famous as the commander of the ill-fated *Apollo 13* mission in 1970, which suffered a serious explosion two days into the flight. Lovell and his crew narrowly survived the disaster and, with help from mission control, returned to Earth safely. In the 1995 movie *Apollo 13*, Lovell was played by Tom Hanks.

SALLY RIDE (1951–2012)

On June 18, 1983, Sally Ride became the first American woman to fly in space. She was a crew member on space shuttle *Challenger* missions, using the robotic arm she helped develop. Back on Earth, she began NASA's EarthKAM project that lets schoolchildren take pictures of Earth using a camera on the International Space Station.

VALENTINA TERESHKOVA (1937–)

Valentina Tereshkova was a Russian parachutist who became an astronaut. On June 16, 1963, she became the first woman to fly in space. During the 70.8-hour flight, her spacecraft *Vostok 6* made 48 orbits of Earth. Soon after liftoff, she had to fix a problem on board. It was discovered that the settings for reentry were wrong and would have sent her out into space rather than back to Earth!

THE INTERNATIONAL SPACE STATION

THE INTERNATIONAL **SPACE STATION** (ISS) IS THE LARGEST SPACECRAFT ORBITING EARTH. ASTRONAUTS AND SCIENTISTS FROM THE UNITED STATES, CANADA, RUSSIA, JAPAN, BRAZIL, AND EUROPE LIVE THERE FOR MONTHS AT A TIME. THEY STUDY SPACE AND ANALYZE HOW THE HUMAN BODY HANDLES LIVING THERE.

The ISS was constructed in space from modules that were delivered piece by piece by 40 missions between 1998 and 2011. Its design was based in part on successful earlier space stations, including Skylab and Mir. The ISS is 243 feet (74 m) long and 360 feet (110 m) wide, which is larger than a football field. On a clear night, you can see the ISS from Earth. It is the third brightest object in the sky, after the sun and moon.

The ISS orbits Earth 16 times a day at a height of around 218 miles (350 km) above Earth's surface. This vast structure would collapse under its own weight if it moved into Earth's atmosphere and experienced our planet's powerful gravity.

" MATH TALK

Shapes matter on the ISS. On Earth, structures like bridges use triangles and beams for strength. The framework of the ISS is made up of many such triangular structures and beams. The modules where astronauts live and work are shaped like cans and spheres. On Earth, fizzy drinks come in cans with no corners weak enough to burst under the pressure of the gassy liquid inside. In space, similar shapes can contain the pressurized atmosphere the astronauts need to breathe and survive.

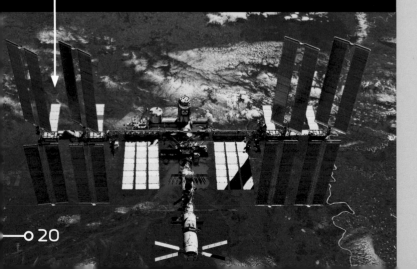

The ISS has about the same amount of room as a five-bedroom house. It can accommodate a crew of six people, plus visitors. Reaching out from the sides of the space station are arms holding wide, flat solar panels. These are designed to capture enough of the sun's energy to supply the ISS with electricity. The ISS also contains small spacecraft that astronauts can use to escape to Earth in case of an emergency.

ENGINEERING TALK

Like space rockets, the ISS is made from very strong and lightweight metals. These include aluminum, titanium, and high-grade steel. Its surface is covered in materials such as Kevlar, the tough stuff used to make bulletproof vests. These materials stop the ISS from being punctured by debris flying around in orbit (see page 13).

THINKING OUTSIDE THE BOX!

Engineers are using the ISS to test ideas for safe structures that humans could live and work in for future trips to more distant destinations. The Bigelow Expandable Activity Module (BEAM) is an inflatable module that has been tested there. These modules are light and small, but after docking with the ISS, they expand to about 13 feet (4 m) long and 10.5 feet (3.2 m) in diameter.

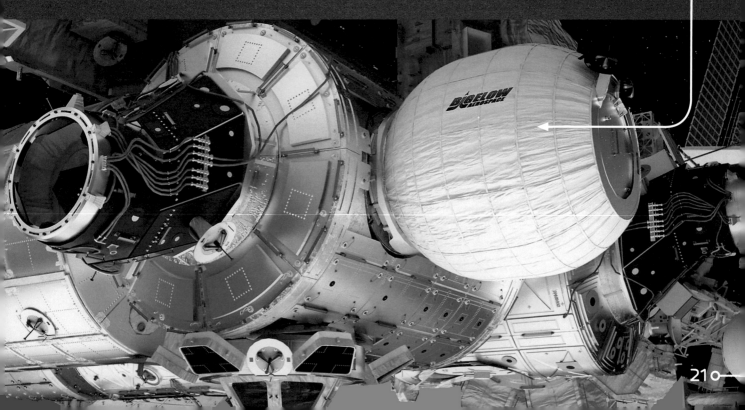

LIVING IN THE STATION

THE INTERNATIONAL SPACE STATION HAS TO PROVIDE EVERYTHING ASTRONAUTS NEED TO SURVIVE IN SPACE. THEY ALSO NEED PROTECTION FROM TEMPERATURE EXTREMES. IT IS ABOUT 200 DEGREES FAHRENHEIT (93 DEGREES CELSIUS) IN THE DAY TO ABOUT MINUS 200 DEGREES FAHRENHEIT (MINUS 129 DEGREES CELSIUS) AT NIGHT!

Temperatures are kept at a comfortable 70°F (21°C) on the ISS, and it is filled with air, so astronauts don't need to wear spacesuits inside. Astronauts float around inside the spacecraft instead of walking. They have to strap themselves to their beds and toilets to prevent them from floating around and crashing into things. They feel weightless because of microgravity (see Science Talk). Astronauts train in **microgravity** conditions for months before going to the ISS.

In microgravity conditions, it is easy for astronauts to move heavy objects because the objects are weightless too. Astronauts can shift big boxes and heavy equipment with just a touch of their fingers.

SCIENCE TALK

Gravity pulls all objects in the same way, no matter how big or small they are. The reason a stone drops faster than a feather when dropped is that air resistance makes the feather fall more slowly. In space there is no air, so the astronauts and the space station are falling at the same speed. This makes astronauts float and feel a less than normal pull of gravity, also known as **microgravity**.

On Earth muscles and bones work against the force of gravity to support and move our bodies. This helps keep them strong. To avoid losing bone mass and muscle strength because of microgravity, astronauts exercise for two or more hours every day. Special straps and elastic cords hold them onto treadmills and bikes and create a downward force for them to push against. With these items, the astronauts don't float away as they exercise.

ENGINEERING TALK

It's expensive to transport water from Earth to the ISS, so recycling is vital. All wastewater is collected, including the astronauts' urine, sweat, and moisture from their breath. The wastewater is filtered to remove impurities and contaminants. This process produces clean water that astronauts use to rehydrate dried food, wash, and drink.

PROJECT

Design a gym for microgravity conditions in space.

- What sort of machines would you include?
- Why do you need to include machines that encourage weight-bearing exercises such as jogging and climbing?
- How would you make weight-lifting possible in microgravity conditions?

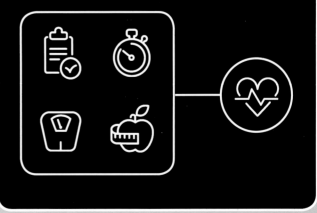

SPACE WALKS

ASTRONAUTS GO ON SPACE WALKS OUTSIDE THE INTERNATIONAL SPACE STATION TO COMPLETE TASKS. THESE TASKS INCLUDE SETTING UP SCIENCE EXPERIMENTS OR MAINTAINING THE SPACECRAFT. ASTRONAUTS ARE TIED TO THE CRAFT BY STRONG SAFETY CORDS TO STOP THEM FROM FLOATING AWAY. THEY ALSO WEAR SPACESUITS FOR PROTECTION.

Spacesuits keep astronauts at a safe, stable temperature. These suits use layers of **insulation** and built-in pipes carrying warm or cool fluids to raise or lower temperatures when needed. The suits contain about 14 layers of different materials. One layer is made of Kevlar to protect the astronauts from space dust and debris. Another layer is waterproof and another is fireproof. Backpacks supply the astronauts with oxygen to breathe and remove the **carbon dioxide** that they breathe out.

TECHNOLOGY TALK

There are at least seven layers of Mylar insulation in most spacesuits. Mylar is a material often used in food storage. It helps maintain an even temperature for astronauts by preventing heat from moving in or out of a spacesuit. This is similar to the way that a Thermos flask or a cooler keeps food and drinks hot or cold.

Astronauts can go on space walks lasting several hours. They pull themselves around using handrails fixed to the exterior of the ISS. They also attach tools and equipment to their spacesuits or the spacecraft. This keeps them from floating away.

A device called a Simplified Aid for Extravehicular Activity Rescue, or SAFER, is attached to the back of each astronauts' spacesuit. This is like a jetpack with several small thruster jets that can be pointed in different directions. The force of gases from a thruster in one direction moves the astronaut in the opposite direction. Thrusters help astronauts get back to the ISS if they become separated from the space station.

SCIENCE TALK

On Earth the weight of air pressing down on us is balanced by **air pressure** in cavities such as our lungs. Because there is no air in space, there is no air pressure. This could cause the gas inside the astronauts' lungs to expand and burst. One layer of each spacesuit contains air that constantly presses against the astronaut's body to maintain a stable level of air pressure.

THINKING OUTSIDE THE BOX!

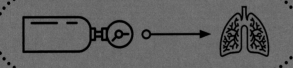

Many of the innovations designed for space have had a big impact on Earth too. The coatings scientists developed for space helmet visors to protect astronauts' eyes from intense sunlight are used for other products. They make the lenses in glasses, sunglasses, and ski goggles 10 times more scratch-resistant than before. Cameras developed to spot infrared light in space are now used to detect forest fires from long distances.

WORKING IN SPACE

MANY JOBS OUTSIDE THE SPACE STATION AND OTHER SPACECRAFT ARE DONE BY ROBOTS RATHER THAN ASTRONAUTS. SPACE WALKS ARE DANGEROUS AND CAN BE EXHAUSTING FOR ASTRONAUTS. ROBOTS DO NOT GET TIRED, CAN DO TOUGHER WORK IN SPACE CONDITIONS, AND ARE REASONABLY EXPENDABLE.

Canadarm2 is a 56-foot (17-m) long robotic arm on the ISS. It can lift about 128 tons (116 tonnes), yet it is made from tough plastic about 13.8 inches (35 cm) in diameter. Canadarm2 can move around like a looping caterpillar. It can plug either of its ends into sockets all over the ISS. The sockets supply power and link to joysticks that astronauts use to control the arm's movements.

Canadarm2 is often used to grab visiting spacecraft to help them dock accurately and safely with the ISS. Astronauts can view and control the exact position of Canadarm2 using video cameras at its joints and ends.

ENGINEERING TALK

Robotic arms are made of several long stiff pieces with joints linking them together that allow the arm to move. In car factories, robotic arms may have just a few parts and simple joints because they are designed to carry out simple movements. Canadarm2 has seven joints, like a human arm. But unlike human elbows and wrist joints, each can rotate fully. This gives Canadarm2 a much wider range of movement.

Canadarm2's strength is used to help unload modules from spacecraft docked to the ISS. It also holds spacewalking astronauts as they carry out more complicated jobs on distant parts of the station. But Canadarm2 isn't the only robot on the ISS. Dextre performs routine tasks on the outside of the ISS, such as changing batteries or connecting cables. Its arms are tipped with tools such as a wrench, drill, light, and camera. Robonaut works inside the ISS. It wipes down handrails to prevent dirt from getting into the air, checks air flow from vents, and completes other tasks.

TECHNOLOGY TALK

Canadarm2 and Dextre have built-in motion and force sensors. Computers in the arms are programmed to monitor and control how much the arms move. Computers also monitor how much force they use based on messages sent from these sensors. This means the astronauts controlling the arm can "feel" how hard it touches or grabs things, and avoid overtightening and damaging nuts and bolts.

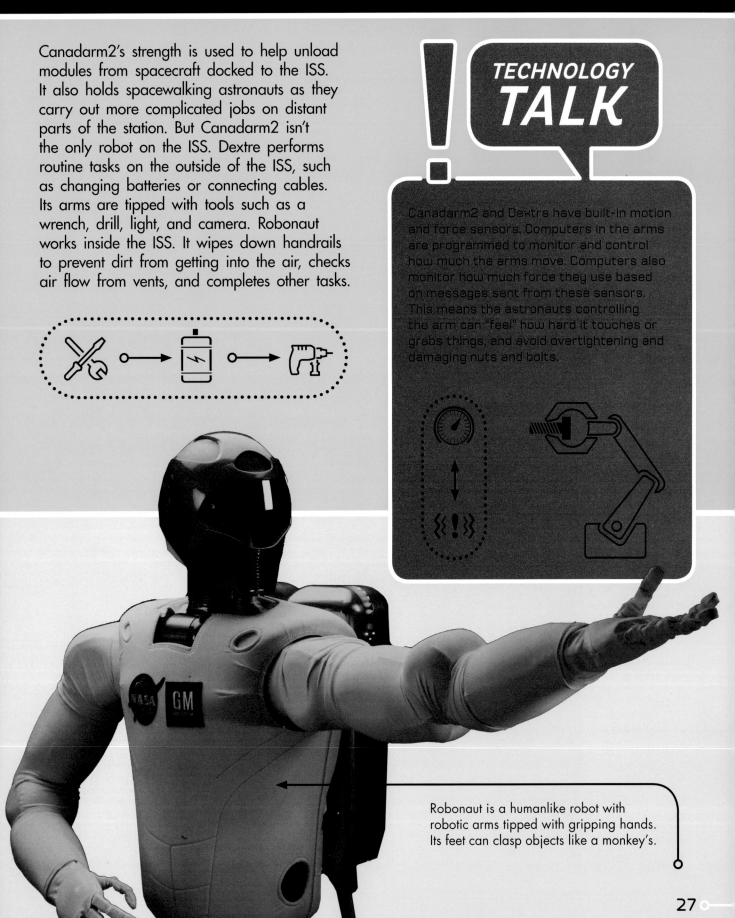

Robonaut is a humanlike robot with robotic arms tipped with gripping hands. Its feet can clasp objects like a monkey's.

SPACE SHUTTLES

COLUMBIA, THE FIRST SPACE SHUTTLE, WAS LAUNCHED IN 1981. IT WAS USED TO TRANSPORT ASTRONAUTS AND SUPPLIES BETWEEN EARTH AND THE ISS. IN 2011 NASA ENDED THE SPACE SHUTTLE PROGRAM TO FOCUS ON OTHER PROJECTS.

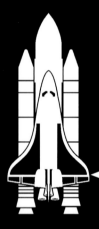

The main part of a shuttle was the **orbiter**, which looked like a plane. This was where astronauts lived and worked. The orbiter was launched from Earth with a blast from its main engine, plus pushes from two solid rocket boosters. These boosters then dropped into the ocean and could be reused. A large, orange external fuel tank attached to the orbiter fueled its trip into orbit. Once empty, the tank fell off and burned upon entering Earth's atmosphere.

TECHNOLOGY TALK

When returning spacecraft get closer to Earth, gravity's pull makes them speed up. Hitting the atmosphere creates friction between speeding metal and air. This friction produces air resistance that helps slow the craft. It also produces enough heat to raise temperatures high enough to melt and burn metal. Discarded rocket stages are left to burn up. Space shuttle orbiters were covered with thousands of tiles made from materials that were not only insulating but also reflected heat. They could withstand temperatures of up to 2,300°F (1,260°C).

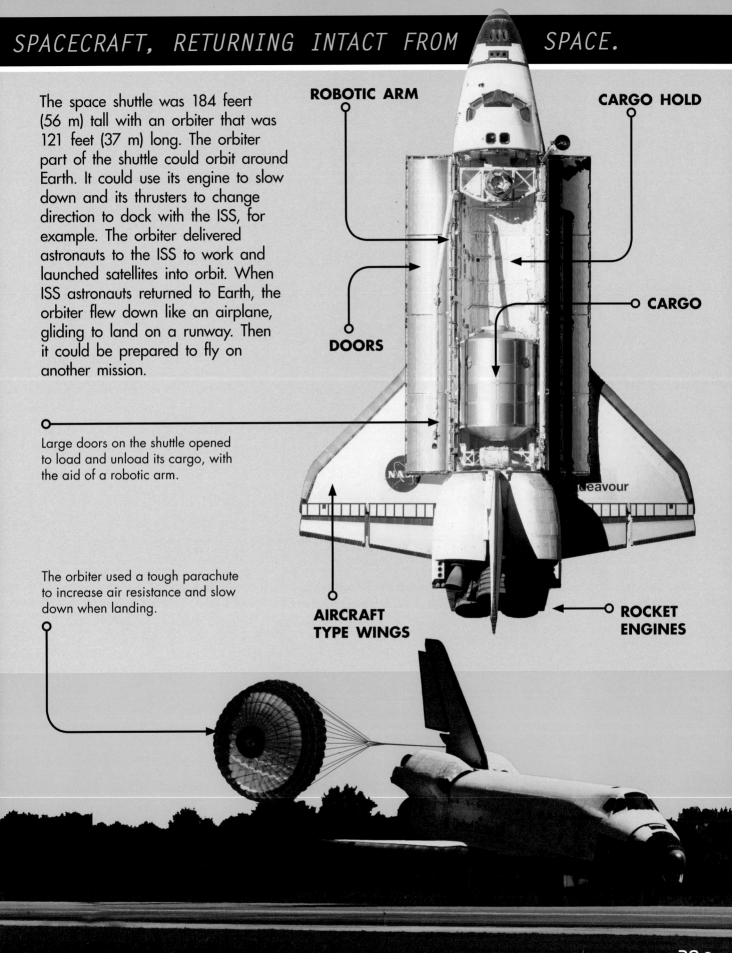

The space shuttle was 184 feert (56 m) tall with an orbiter that was 121 feet (37 m) long. The orbiter part of the shuttle could orbit around Earth. It could use its engine to slow down and its thrusters to change direction to dock with the ISS, for example. The orbiter delivered astronauts to the ISS to work and launched satellites into orbit. When ISS astronauts returned to Earth, the orbiter flew down like an airplane, gliding to land on a runway. Then it could be prepared to fly on another mission.

ROBOTIC ARM

CARGO HOLD

CARGO

DOORS

Large doors on the shuttle opened to load and unload its cargo, with the aid of a robotic arm.

The orbiter used a tough parachute to increase air resistance and slow down when landing.

AIRCRAFT TYPE WINGS

ROCKET ENGINES

SINCE THE DAWN OF SPACE EXPLORATION, SCIENTISTS AND ENGINEERS HAVE COME UP WITH A VARIETY OF AMAZING SPACECRAFT THAT HAVE HELPED HUMANS EXPLORE SPACE.

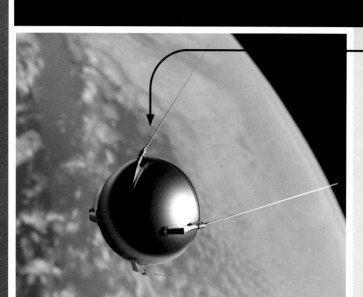

SPUTNIK 1

On October 4, 1957, *Sputnik 1* became the first spacecraft to orbit Earth. It was a simple artificial satellite about the same size as a basketball. It was launched by the Soviet Union, and its name is Russian for "traveling companion." *Sputnik 1* circled Earth every 96 minutes until early 1958. Then it fell back toward Earth and burned up in the atmosphere.

APOLLO 11

Apollo 11 was the first spacecraft to land men on the moon. It launched from Florida on July 16, 1969, using a Saturn V rocket. *Apollo 11* had a command module, where astronauts stayed for the flight. It also had a lunar module that they used to explore the moon's surface.

MIR SPACE STATION

The Russian space station Mir operated from 1986 to 2000. Traveling at an average speed of about 17,885 miles (28,783 km) per hour, Mir orbited about 250 miles (400 km) above Earth for nearly 15 years. Astronauts aboard Mir used seeds to grow the first crop of wheat in space!

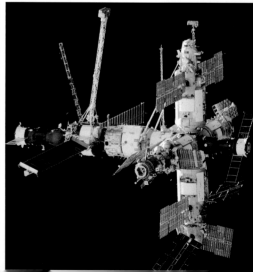

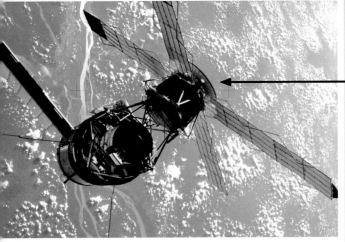

SKYLAB

Skylab was the first U.S. space station. It launched into Earth's orbit on May 14, 1973. Skylab was 99 feet (30 m) long and 22 feet (6.7 m) in diameter. After being visited by three crews, it started to degrade in the sun's rays. In July 1979 it entered Earth's atmosphere and broke apart. Pieces of it fell into the Indian Ocean and across Australia.

SPACE SHUTTLE *CHALLENGER*

NASA had five space shuttle orbiters: *Atlantis, Challenger, Columbia, Discovery,* and *Endeavour. Challenger* first launched in 1983 and completed nine missions, including the one that took the first female U.S. astronaut, Sally Ride, into space. Sadly, it is most famous for its tenth mission, in January 1986, when a booster seal failed and hot gas burned through the external tank. This caused a fatal explosion that killed the seven astronauts on board.

SPACEX DRAGON V2

The 23-foot (7.2-m) tall SpaceX Dragon V2 is designed to carry astronauts to Earth's orbit and beyond. The first Dragon has been carrying cargo to and from the ISS since 2012. Dragon V2 has a capsule that can carry both cargo and seven passengers into space. It can land almost anywhere on Earth, refuel, and fly off again quickly.

SPACE TELESCOPES [+]

ASTRONOMERS USE POWERFUL OPTICAL TELESCOPES ON EARTH TO VIEW STARS AND PLANETS. AND THEY CAN GET A FAR CLEARER IMAGE BY USING SPACE TELESCOPES THAT BEAM BACK THEIR REMARKABLE VIEW.

The night sky is rarely dark on Earth because of light pollution from streetlights, homes, and cars. This makes dimly lit distant objects in space harder to spot. Our atmosphere is also made from moving air that bends or **refracts** the light from space so objects are less clear. This is the reason why stars appear to twinkle. These effects are reduced by building observatories on high ground in places with less light pollution. Making telescopes that use special mirrors also helps reduce the refraction of light from space.

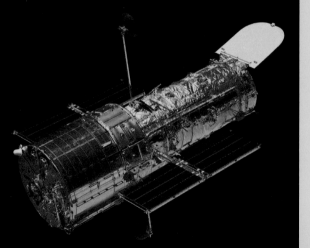

Hubble has been observing the far reaches of space from 353.5 miles (569 km) above Earth since 1990.

In space, telescopes can get a clearer shot of everything because there is no light pollution. Space telescopes, such as the Hubble Telescope, detect not only visible light but also invisible light, such as ultraviolet and infrared. Other space telescopes can even detect the faint **X-rays** produced by galaxies billions of light years away. Images are sent back to Earth from space telescopes as data signals that are reconstructed into images by powerful computers.

SCIENCE TALK

Warm objects such as the sun give off infrared light, or heat. The clearest way to view stars and planets far away is by using the infrared light they emit, rather than visible light. Scientists have devised sensors on space telescopes that can detect even tiny amounts of infrared radiation. Such technology is useless on Earth's telescopes because the atmosphere absorbs most of this radiation.

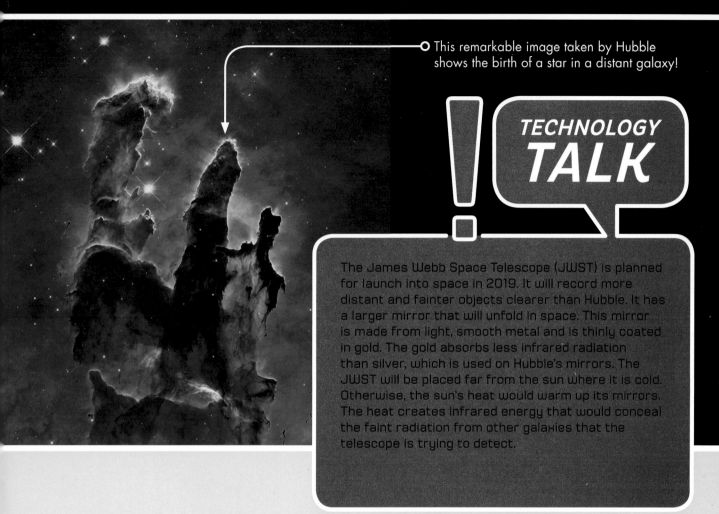

This remarkable image taken by Hubble shows the birth of a star in a distant galaxy!

TECHNOLOGY TALK

The James Webb Space Telescope (JWST) is planned for launch into space in 2019. It will record more distant and fainter objects clearer than Hubble. It has a larger mirror that will unfold in space. This mirror is made from light, smooth metal and is thinly coated in gold. The gold absorbs less infrared radiation than silver, which is used on Hubble's mirrors. The JWST will be placed far from the sun where it is cold. Otherwise, the sun's heat would warm up its mirrors. The heat creates infrared energy that would conceal the faint radiation from other galaxies that the telescope is trying to detect.

MATH TALK

Hexagons are shapes that fit together without gaps. They occur naturally in wax honeycombs made by bees, but the shapes are also used in the JWST's mirror segments. Individual motors tilt each mirror by amounts as small as thousandths of a human hair's thickness. This helps focus light exactly onto the JWST's sensors.

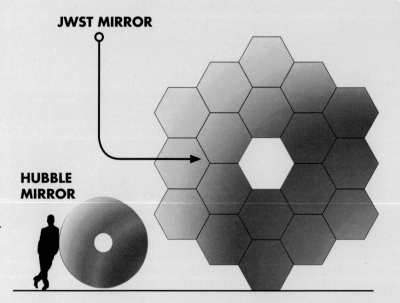

JWST MIRROR

HUBBLE MIRROR

OVER TIME, PEOPLE STUDYING SPACE HAVE DISCOVERED MORE AND MORE ABOUT THE AMAZING SPACE PHENOMENA FOUND IN THE UNIVERSE.

HALL OF FAME: SPACE PHENOMENA

BLACK HOLE

A black hole is an area in space where gravity is so strong that even light cannot escape. Gravity is very powerful in a black hole because a lot of matter is compressed into a small space. One such example is when a star dies and collapses in on itself. Black holes themselves are invisible, but scientists can see their effects.

DWARF PLANET

A dwarf planet is a huge, spherical, natural object that orbits the sun just like other planets. But it is much smaller. Dwarf planets are generally less than one-third the size of Earth. Pluto was considered a full planet until 2006. Then experts reclassified it as a dwarf planet because they found its gravity was too weak to pull smaller nearby objects toward it. This pull is a requirement for planets.

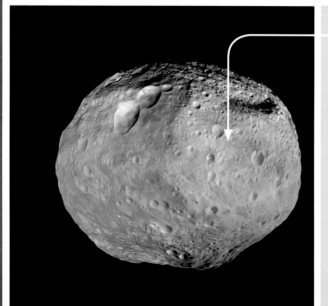

ASTEROID

Asteroids are rocks that orbit the sun and are up to 373 miles (600 km) wide but are too small to be called planets. Asteroids were left over from the Big Bang 4.5 billion years ago (see pages 4–5). About once a year, an asteroid as big as a car enters Earth's atmosphere. It ignites into a fireball and burns up before reaching Earth's surface.

METEOROID

Meteoroids are fragments of space rock that orbit the sun. Most meteoroids burn up in a flash of light, sometimes forming a meteor shower when they enter Earth's atmosphere. People often call them "shooting stars." Any meteoroids that hit Earth are called meteorites. Once every 2,000 years or so, a meteorite as big as a football field touches down somewhere on Earth! This can create massive craters and throw up giant dust clouds.

COMET

A comet is a gigantic ball of ice, dust, and rock that orbits the sun. If it strays too close to the sun, the ice inside it condenses into gas. This forms the glowing tail we see in the night sky when a comet passes over. Many comets take hundreds or thousands of years to orbit the sun, and very rarely pass near Earth. The famous Halley's comet is a more regular visitor, appearing every 74–79 years!

SUPERNOVA

The biggest explosion that happens in space is when a star blows up. It is called a supernova. A supernova creates so much light that it can burn brighter than a whole galaxy of stars. It also releases more energy than our sun ever will. Supernovas are important because they release matter such as carbon and iron throughout space. Almost everything on Earth is made up of these elements.

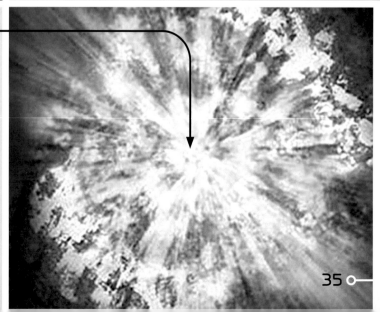

PROBES AND ORBITERS

PROBES ARE ROBOTIC VEHICLES THAT TAKE ONE-WAY TRIPS TO COLLECT SCIENTIFIC DATA FROM THE UNIVERSE. ORBITERS ARE LIKE PROBES BUT ARE DESIGNED TO ORBIT PLANETS OR MOONS TO STUDY THEM IN GREATER DETAIL.

Probes are carried into space as rocket payload. They separate from the rocket and automatically follow courses programmed into their onboard computers. They can often be controlled using signals from operators on Earth too. When they reach their destination, they relay information to Earth through radio signals. This includes pictures taken by onboard cameras and data such as size of planetary features, temperatures, and wind speeds in space.

This drawing shows the Voyager 1 probe. The two Voyager probes have traveled nonstop since they were launched in 1977. They travel at speeds of over 34,000 miles (55,000 km) per hour. Both send data about space back to Earth.

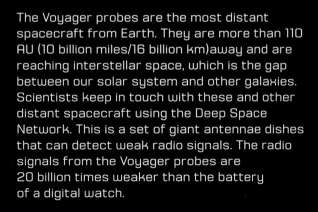

SCIENCE TALK

The Voyager probes are the most distant spacecraft from Earth. They are more than 110 AU (10 billion miles/16 billion km) away and are reaching interstellar space, which is the gap between our solar system and other galaxies. Scientists keep in touch with these and other distant spacecraft using the Deep Space Network. This is a set of giant antennae dishes that can detect weak radio signals. The radio signals from the Voyager probes are 20 billion times weaker than the battery of a digital watch.

Orbiters circle near planets multiple times to take sequences of close-up images that show changes. These changes might be volcanic eruptions or shifting cloud patterns. Sensors collect detailed data, such as the chemical composition of atmospheres around other planets. Probes and orbiters have discovered amazing things. For example, Jupiter has more than 60 moons, some with active volcanoes, and Saturn has wind speeds of more than 1,056 miles (1,700 km) per hour.

Cameras on the Cassini orbiter took this incredibly detailed image of Saturn's rings in 2013.

THINKING OUTSIDE THE BOX!

Probes and orbiters traveling to destinations near the sun use solar panels to produce power to move and run their instruments. But vehicles visiting the outer gas planets are moving away from the sun, where the sun's strength is weaker. Therefore, engineers install engines on these vehicles that convert the heat from nuclear power packs into electricity. Then they can carry on working in the darkness of space.

MATH TALK

Mathematicians help probes and orbiters reduce travel time by calculating ways for them to hop between planetary orbits. Planets have different sizes and speeds of orbit around the sun. It makes sense to time the trip for when they have moved closest together. A spacecraft to Mars, for example, can loop several times around Earth, accelerating faster and faster using gravity. Then, at a precisely calculated time, it exits this orbit at speed to meet up with Mars' orbit. This process is called gravity assist.

LANDERS AND ROVERS

PROBES AND ORBITERS GO CLOSE TO OBJECTS IN SPACE, BUT LANDERS ACTUALLY TOUCH DOWN ON THEM. SOME CARRY VEHICLES CALLED ROVERS DESIGNED TO EXPLORE THE OBJECT AFTER ARRIVAL. BOTH ROBOTIC MACHINES HELP PEOPLE ON EARTH KNOW MORE ABOUT SURFACE CONDITIONS ELSEWHERE IN THE SOLAR SYSTEM.

Landers need to be tough to survive the descent. They may have to pass through poisonous gases or sizzlingly hot atmospheres around planets such as Mars. Then they must reduce speed from very fast to a standstill without crashing. Landers gain as much information as possible about the area they land in. For example, they use robotic arms to scoop up soil, which they test for chemicals. Cameras take detailed images of the surface to help them map features such as hills, craters, and valleys.

Sky Crane was an object that lowered the rover *Curiosity* to the surface of Mars. It hit Mars' atmosphere at 13,049 miles (21,000 km) per hour and used air resistance, a parachute, and downward-pointing thrusters to slow down to 1.5 miles (2.4 km) per hour. Then it lowered *Curiosity* safely to the surface on ropes, before flying away and self-destructing.

PROJECT

Design a lander to carry a delicate object, such as an egg, from up in the air to the ground without damage.

- What system(s) would you use to slow the descent?
- What material could cushion the landing?
- How could you protect the object inside from high or low temperatures?

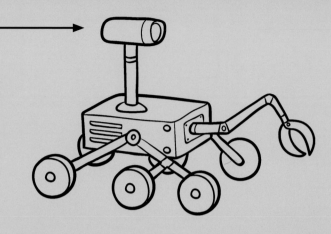

Rovers get images and data from a much wider area than landers because they can move around. They often transmit data to their lander, which may be orbiting the planet and can communicate with Earth. These tough motorized vehicles vary in size from a microwave oven to a car. Some are steered using signals from Earth but others navigate themselves.

The first rover was driven by astronauts on moon missions. Today's rovers are robots that move automatically across other planets and even comets.

TECHNOLOGY TALK

Operators on Earth send map references of rover destinations. But a rover's onboard computer calculates the best route by comparing images taken by its cameras with stored maps and necessary data. If it meets unexpected obstacles, operators calculate and transmit the best route. The rover also learns how to deal with similar problems for the future. Engineers are using similar technology to develop driverless vehicles on Earth.

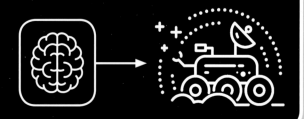

" MATH TALK

In 2014 the Philae lander touched down on a speeding comet. The spacecraft carrying it (Rosetta) had left Earth in 2004. Mathematicians had to calculate where the comet was going to be 10 years ahead of time and spot a landing opportunity. Philae took seven hours to land after it was released from Rosetta, and its speed was very carefully controlled. If its speed was off, it could have missed the target and fallen off the comet.

CURIOSITY

CURIOSITY IS THE MOST ADVANCED ROVER EVER BUILT. SINCE LANDING ON MARS IN 2012 (SEE PAGE 38), THE DATA IT HAS COLLECTED HAS HELPED SCIENTISTS GET ALMOST FIRSTHAND KNOWLEDGE OF THE PLANET.

Curiosity is the size of a small car. On top, it has a mast with cameras so scientists on Earth can see where it is going and what it is doing. It has a **laser** to blast rocks and sensors to detect what chemicals they contain. If they are of interest to scientists, operators command Curiosity to stretch out its robotic arm to collect a sample. Samples are used to analyze in more detail.

Curiosity's 2015 selfie shows the rocky terrain of the large Mars crater where it landed. It is still exploring that crater to this day.

ENGINEERING TALK

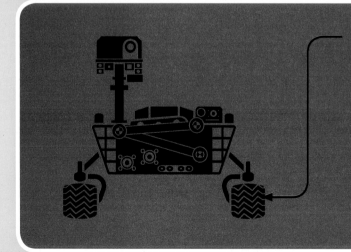

Curiosity is engineered to handle the dusty soil and bumpy terrain of Mars. It has six large wheels with thick treads or grooves to increase friction. Each wheel has its own motor to move the rover in all directions. It also has a suspension system so springy that Curiosity can drive over obstacles more than 2 feet (65 cm) high. It can do this while keeping all six wheels on the ground for stability.

a dried up ancient lake on Mars

One of Curiosity's tasks is to look for signs of life on Mars. Until 2014 there was no evidence. But then Curiosity sampled methane in the atmosphere. This gas contains carbon, which is a substance most living things contain. Curiosity also unearthed carbon-rich chemicals in sandy rocks on the planet. The carbon could have come from space dust, but on Earth, it is usually made by living things called **bacteria**. Could this be proof of life on the red planet?

ART TALK

David Hockney and other artists have produced images made from lots of overlapping photos. These are called photomontages. Each is taken from a slightly different viewpoint. The pictures are combined to create a different image than one produced from a single viewpoint. Mars teams have constructed wide-angle "selfie" views of Curiosity and its terrain in a similar way. The teams piece together dozens of different photos taken by a camera on its arm.

Curiosity's arm tip includes many tools. These include a grinder to drill holes in rocks, a spectrometer to test quantities of chemicals in rocks, and a microscope for close viewing. Another sensor onboard is like an artificial nose to check the gases in the atmosphere. Curiosity moves very slowly and is methodical in its work. In five years on the planet, it covered just 9.3 miles (15 km).

PROJECT

Produce a self-portrait using a montage of overlapping photos of your face.

- Try using some close-ups and some wide-angle shots from varying viewpoints.
- Think of how you could show the passage of time or family resemblances in a photomontage.

SPACE COLONIES

THERE ARE MANY REASONS WHY PEOPLE HAVE EXPLORED SPACE SO FAR. THE PRIMARY REASON IS KNOWING MORE ABOUT THE UNIVERSE AND LOOKING FOR SIGNS OF OTHER LIFE. THIS QUEST WOULD HAVE BEEN IMPOSSIBLE WITHOUT CUTTING-EDGE SCIENCE, TECHNOLOGY, ENGINEERING, ART, AND MATH SKILLS TO SOLVE PROBLEMS. NOW PEOPLE ARE USING THEIR KNOWLEDGE OF SPACE TO PLAN FOR THE NEXT STEP—HUMAN COLONIES ON OTHER PLANETS.

Earth is good at supporting life as we know it. It has an oxygen-rich atmosphere, a range of temperatures that living things can handle, supplies of water, and other natural resources. However, demand from an increasing human population is putting pressure on these resources and causing other problems, such as pollution.

Probes, orbiters, and rovers have proven that Mars is the nearest planet most resembling Earth. It is rocky, has ice and other signs of water, and its rocks contain mineral resources, such as iron. This resource is useful for building. However, the atmosphere is mostly carbon dioxide, it is colder than Antarctica, and it has planetwide dust storms. Technological solutions will be needed to melt Mars' ice for drinking water, produce oxygen, and warm buildings to grow plants for food. But life on Mars may one day be possible.

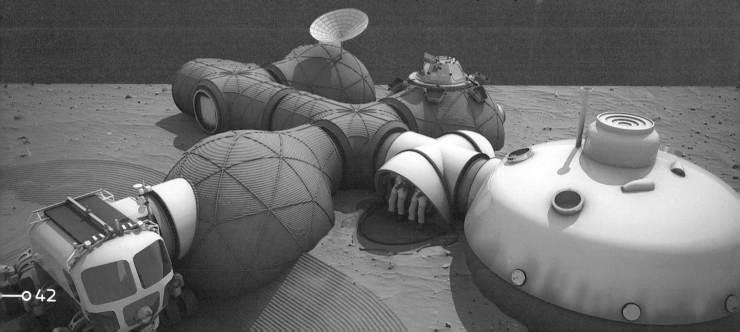

TECHNOLOGY TALK

Mars is over 35 million miles (56 million km) from Earth. The farthest humans have traveled is around 250,000 miles (400,000 km) from Earth. With current rockets, it would take about nine months for a human mission to reach Mars. Plus the launch vehicle, lander, fuel, crew, water, and other life support for a complete mission would be enormous in weight. The weight is greater than even the newest heavy-lifter launch vehicles could carry. So the only solution is to construct and take supplies to the Mars mission craft while it is in orbit.

The Space Launch System includes a rocket and the Orion spacecraft. This new system can lift 143 tons (130 tonnes) of cargo. It is planned for use in 2021. Orion eventually will be used for a test trip to Mars and back to Earth, which will kick-start a new era of Mars exploration.

THINKING OUTSIDE THE BOX!

Towering termite mounds are constructed by millions of insects coordinating their efforts to make single complex structures. Scientists are inspired by this cooperation in developing mini-robots capable of digging and constructing in teams on Mars and other planets. For example, if one robot places its brick in one location, the next uses visual clues and its programming to put its brick next to it. Or the robot puts the brick on top of it or elsewhere that helps build the final construction.

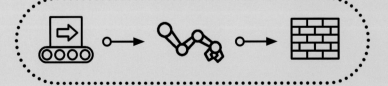

SPACE TOURISM

SPACE TRAVEL IS USUALLY RESERVED FOR HIGHLY TRAINED ASTRONAUTS. BUT A NEW WAVE OF SPACESHIPS COULD BE TAKING TOURISTS TO SPACE IN THE VERY NEAR FUTURE.

In the next few years, space tourism companies hope to start taking paying passengers beyond Earth's atmosphere. Fully trained astronauts would fly the spacecraft, taking tourists on a trip lasting about 90 minutes, up to 100 miles (160 km) above Earth. There, the tourists will experience several minutes of weightlessness and a clear view of the stars above and the planet Earth below.

TECHNOLOGY TALK

Space tourism is currently only really an option for the super-rich. In the future, new technology will allow anyone to view the wonders of space from their armchair. A satellite with wide field-of-view cameras and sensors will beam live images of space and Earth to virtual reality headsets.

One company working with the Russian national space agency has already taken passengers for 10-day trips to the ISS. The cost is more than $20 million each. Now private companies are testing new tourist spaceship designs. Virgin Galactic's *SpaceShipTwo* is a spacecraft with wings that can carry up to eight people, including pilots, into space over and over again. Anyone who takes such a flight automatically receives official astronaut status.

SpaceShipTwo doesn't launch from the ground like most rockets. A jet aircraft carries it more than 9 miles (15 km) in the air. Then it ignites its rocket engine and takes off on its own.

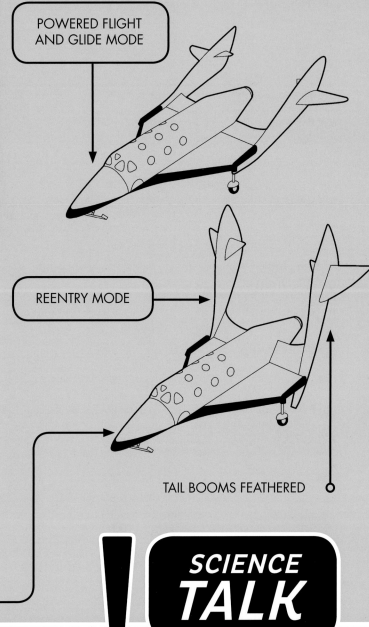

POWERED FLIGHT AND GLIDE MODE

REENTRY MODE

TAIL BOOMS FEATHERED

THINKING OUTSIDE THE BOX!

SpaceShipTwo can work like a space capsule or a winged vehicle at different times during its flight. To safely reenter Earth's atmosphere, it can reposition its wings. The tail booms move from a horizontal position to a 65-degree upright angle. This is known as feathering, and it helps to slow down the spacecraft during its descent. Then the tail booms return to their normal position so *SpaceShipTwo* can glide down to land on a runway.

SCIENCE TALK

During rocket launches, carbon dioxide gas is emitted when the fuel is burned. The gas and soot emitted by the rockets store the sun's heat and warm the atmosphere. This is one way that global warming is raising average temperatures on Earth and contributing to changing weather patterns and melting polar ice. Increased global warming and climate change could be a consequence of increased space tourism in the future.

GLOSSARY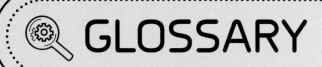

aerodynamic (ayr-oh-dy-NA-mik)—designed to reduce air resistance

air pressure (AYR PRESH-ur)—the weight of air pushing against something

air resistance (AYR ri-ZISS-tuhnss)—the force of air rubbing against things; air resistance slows down moving vehicles, such as cars and airplanes

asteroid (AS-tuh-royd)—a chunk of rock and metal left over from the solar system's formation

atmosphere (AT-muhss-fear)—a blanket of gases that surround a planet

bacteria (bak-TEER-ee-uh)—single-celled microscopic creatures that exist everywhere in nature

black hole (BLAK HOHL)—an area of space with such a strong gravitational field that not even light can escape from it

carbon dioxide (KAHR-buhn dy-AHK-syd)—a gas in the air that animals give off and plants use to make food

comet (KOM-uht)—an icy, dusty object that orbits a star

drag (DRAG)—the force created when air strikes a moving object; drag slows down moving objects

escape velocity (es-KAYP vuh-LOSS-uh-tee)—the speed an object needs to reach in order to escape the gravity of another object

force (FORS)—the push or pull on an object that results from its interaction with another object

friction (FRIK-shuhn)—a force produced whenbtwo objects rub against each other; friction slows objects

galaxy (GAL-uhk-see)—a cluster of gas, dust, and millions of stars, bound together by gravity

Global Positioning System (GPS) (GLOH-buhl puh-ZI-shuh-ning SISS-tuhm)—an electronic tool used to find the location of an object

gravity (GRAV-uh-tee)—a force that pulls objects together

helium (HEE-lee-uhm)—a gas that is lighter than air

insulation (in-suh-LAY-shun)—a material that stops heat, sound, or cold from entering or escaping

laser (LAY-zur)—an intense, high-energy beam of light

mass (MASS)—the amount of material in an object

microgravity (mye-kruh-GRAV-uh-tee)—very weak gravity that creates a feeling of weightlessness

orbit (OR-bit)—the path of a planet or star around a larger body like the sun

orbiter (OR-bit-ur)—an unmanned spacecraft that flies in orbit around a planet collecting images and data

oxygen (OK-suh-juhn)—a gas in air that living things need to breathe in order to live

payload (PAY-lohd)—the weight of items carried by a plane or other vehicle

probe (PROHB)—a spacecraft sent to gather data

propulsion (proh-PUHL-shuhn)—the thrust or power that makes an airplane or rocket move forward

radiation (ray-dee-AY-shuhn)—rays of energy given off by certain elements

refract (ri-FRACT)—to bend light as it passes through a substance at an angle

satellite (SAT-uh-lite)—an electronic device or object, such as the moon, high in space that moves around Earth

sensor (SEN-sur)—a device that detects changes in heat, light, sound, or motion

Soviet Union (SOH-vee-et YOON-yuhn)—a former federation of 15 republics that included Russia, and other nations of eastern Europe and northern Asia

space station (SPAYSS STAY-shuhn)—a large spacecraft that remains in orbit

streamlined (STREEM-lined)—designed to move easily and quickly through air or water

thrust (THRUHST)—the force that pushes a vehicle forward

thruster (THRUHST-ur)—an engine that produces forward momentum by discharging a jet of fluid or a stream of particles

X-ray (EKS-ray)—a type of radiation that can pass through most materials

READ MORE

Becker, Helaine. *Everything Space*. National Geographic Kids. Washington, D.C.: National Geographic Society, 2015.

Russo, Kristin J. *Space*. Facts or Fibs? North Mankato, Minn.: Capstone Press, 2018.

INTERNET SITES

Use FactHound to find Internet sites related to this book.

Visit www.facthound.com

Just type in 9781543532364 and go.

Check out projects, games and lots more at
www.capstonekids.com

QUIZ

INDEX

QUIZ ANSWERS

- Robert Goddard

- They are too far from the sun to get enough light.

- Moving around one planet using its gravity to orbit and build speed to jump to another orbit

- Yuri Gagarin and Neil Armstrong

- There is less light pollution, atmospheric interference, and absorption of infrared radiation.